2000

by PABLO NERUDA

DEA·74

2000

by PABLO NERUDA

Translated by Richard Schaaf

Introduction by Fernando Alegría

Azul Editions
Washington, D.C.

This bilingual edition published by
Azul Editions
2032 Belmont Rd., N.W., Suite 301
Washington, D.C. 20009 USA

ISBN 0-9632363-0-X
Library of Congress Catalogue Number: 92-70941

Frontispiece: Dea Trier Mørch

First North American Edition
Printed in the United States of America

Introduction

No one, as far as I know, has acknowledged that *2000* is Neruda's book of divinations, his missal of presentiments and his prayer book of survival.

So visionary is the poet's intuition! Struck down by the lightning bolt of tyrannized hatred, dead and buried among the ruins of his house of odes, shipwrecked from his sea shells in Isla Negra, submerged and sustained by Chile's roots under the sea, under the snow and under time that has circled round from zero to zero — until arriving at the year 2000 — Neruda observes the mystery of history and illuminates it with simplicity and candor, force and daring, ready to celebrate and crown the new century with three zeros.

Let us not forget: Neruda foresaw the political precipice of the 1990s — the collapse of the walls of the cold war, the twilight of dictators, the dark night of dogmatism, the sad emptiness of reformists — and calmly and ardently he saluted the universal conscience of the new century on the horizon:

Pity on these centuries and their happy or
battered survivors, what we did not do
was the fault of no one, steel was missing:
we exhausted it on so much useless destruction
but none of this matters in the balance . . . .

The impatient gravediggers, as soon as the Berlin Wall fell, stormed into the streets with their shovels to bury the hair-raising specter of utopias. The summer fools, they cried out, frowning: It is the end of history!

Neruda answers them with an enigmatic smile on his lips:

Praised be the old land the color of excrement,
its cavities, its sacrosanct ovaries,
the storehouses of wisdom that contained
copper, oil, magnets, ironworks, purity,
the lightning bolt that seemed to fall from hell
was hoarded by the ancient mother of roots
and each day bread came out to greet us . . . .

Neruda never found reason to abandon his humanism; he fought, he lost, he won, he disappeared amid the clamor of violent deaths, executions, tortures and book burnings, and still his enormous smile was not erased from his face, and still hope continued breathing life in his demolished house in Santiago:

I want to leave my grave — I, a dead man —
    why not?

Why do those born before their time go on being
    forgotten?
Everyone is invited to the party! . . .

and we, death's representatives,
we want to exist for one single flowering moment
when the doors to a future with dignity and honor
    open!

Neruda took the long and arduous road of the materialist philosophers who visit life and become enamored of the passing of each season, and who come to the end of life's journey singing of golden autumns. Full of hope, from his memorial in another world, he triumphantly claims his place in the future and announces his participation in the human struggle to achieve the longed-for peace of a new history, the heartfelt embrace of three equal, commonly shared zeros:

> Not even Florence knew a more flourishing
> Age, more flowering than Florida,
> more Paradise than Valparaíso.
> Now I can breathe comfortably
> in the financial garden of this century
> that is finally a great bank account
> in which I am, luckily, a creditor.

2000 is an oracular and jubilant poem in which a removed hero, but by no means gone from the scene, weighs in the balance the cold war and fiery hatreds in order to tell us that History has not ended: it is just being born with a new, unexpected and wondrous heartthrob.

— Fernando Alegría

Las Máscaras

The Masks

Piedad para estos siglos y sus
        sobrevivientes
alegres o maltrechos, lo que no hicimos
fue por culpa de nadie, faltó acero:
lo gastamos en tanta inútil destrucción,
no importa en el balance nada de esto:
los años padecieron de pústulas y guerras,
años desfallecientes cuando tembló la
        esperanza
en el fondo de las botellas enemigas.

Pity on these centuries and their
        happy
or battered survivors, what we did not do
was the fault of no one, steel was missing:
we exhausted it on so much destruction,
but none of this matters in the balance:
the years suffered from oozing sores and wars,
years grown weak when hope trembled
at the bottom of the enemy's bottles.

Muy bien, hablaremos alguna vez, algunas
        veces,
con una golondrina para que nadie
        escuche:
tengo vergüenza, tenemos el pudor de los
        viudos:
se murió la verdad y se pudrió en tantas
        fosas:
es mejor recordar lo que va a suceder:
en este año nupcial no hay derrotados:
pongámonos cada uno máscaras
        victoriosas.

Very well, we will talk sometime,
        sometimes,
with a swallow so that no one
        can listen:
I am ashamed, we possess the humble
        decency of widows:
truth died and rotted in so many
        graves:
it is best to remember what is going to happen:
in this nuptial year there are no defeated ones:
let each one of us put on victorious
        masks.

Las Invenciones

The Inventions

Ves este pequeño objeto trisilábico?
Es un cilindro subalterno de la felicidad
y manejado, ahora, por organismos
          coherentes
desde control remoto, estoy, estad seguros
de una eficacia tan resplandeciente
que maduran las uvas a su presión ignota
y el trigo a pleno campo se convierte en
          pan,
las yeguas dan a luz caballos bermellones
que galopan el aire sin previo aviso,
grandes industrias se mueven como
          escolopendras
dejando ruedas y relojes en los sitios
          inhabitados:

Do you see this small trisyllabic object?
It is a secondary cylinder of happiness
and operated, now, by coherent
          organisms
from remote control — I am sure, you be assured
of an efficacy so resplendent
that grapes ripen under its as yet unknown
          pressure
and fields of wheat are turned to
          bread,
mares give birth to vermilion horses
that suddenly rear up and gallop on the wind,
enormous industries move like
          centipedes
leaving behind wheels and clocks in uninhabited
          places:

Señores, adquirid mi producto terciario
sin mezcla de algodón ni de sustancias
      lácteas:
os concedo un botón para cambiar el
      mundo:
adquirid el trifásico antes de arrepentirme!

Gentlemen, acquire my tertiary product,
pure, free of cotton or milky
            substances:
I grant you a button in order to transform
            the world:
acquire my three-phase current before I regret it!

Las Espigas

Spikes of Wheat

El sin cesar ha terminado en flores,
en largo tiempo que extiende su camino
en cinta, en la novedad del aire,
y si por fin hallamos bajo el polvo
el mecanismo del próximo futuro
simplemente reconozcamos la alegría
así como se presenta! Como una espiga
   más,
de tal manera que el olvido contribuya
a la claridad verdadera que sin duda no
   existe.

The ceaseless turning has ended in flowers,
in a long time stretching its road
all around, into the air's newness,
and if at last we find under the dust
the mechanism for the next future
let us simply recognize happiness
as soon as it shows itself! As one more
        spike of wheat,
in such a way that oblivion contributes
to true clarity, which no doubt does not
        exist.

La Tierra

The Earth

Amarillo, amarillo sigue siendo
el perro que detrás del otoño circula
haciendo entre las hojas circunferencias
        de oro,
ladrando hacia los días desconocidos.
Así veréis lo imprevisto de ciertas
        situaciones:
junto al explorador de las terribles
        fronteras
que abren el infinito, he aquí el predilecto,
el animal perdido del otoño.
Qué puede cambiar de tierra a tiempo, de
        sabor a estribor,
de luz velocidad a circunstancia terrestre?

The dog that backtracks in autumn,
tracing golden circumferences among the
        leaves,
barking toward unknown days,
continues being yellow, yellow.
So shall you see the unforseen in certain
        situations:
beside the explorer of terrible
        frontiers
that open to the infinite, here is my dog:
autumn's stray animal.
How can one move from earth to time, from
        a savor to starboard,
from the speed of light to earthly circumstance?

Quién adivinará la semilla en la sombra
si como cabelleras las mismas arboledas
dejan caer rocío sobre las mismas
          herraduras,
sobre las cabezas que reúne el amor,
sobre las cenizas de corazones muertos?
Este mismo planeta, la alfombra de mil
          años,
puede florecer pero no acepta la muerte
          ni el reposo:
las cíclicas cerraduras de la fertilidad
se abren en cada primavera para las llaves
          del sol
y resuenan los frutos haciéndose cascada,
sube y baja el fulgor de la tierra a la boca
y el humano agradece la bondad de su
          reino.

Who in the darkness will divine the seed
if, like strands of hair, the leafy groves
let fall dew
       on horseshoes,
on heads that love unites,
on the ashes of worn out hearts?
This planet, carpet thousands of years
       old,
shall flourish but it does not accept death
       nor repose:
each spring the sun's keys open
fertility's cyclical locks,
and cascading bunches of fruit resound,
the earth's splendor rises and falls to the mouth
and humankind is thankful for the goodness of
       its kingdom.

Alabada sea la vieja tierra color de
        excremento,
sus cavidades, sus ovarios sacrosantos,
las bodegas de la sabiduría que encerraron
cobre, petróleo, imanes, ferreterías, pureza,
el relámpago que parecía bajar desde el
        infierno
fue atesorado por la antigua madre de las
        raíces
y cada día salió el pan a saludarnos
sin importarle la sangre y la muerte que
        vestimos los hombres,
la maldita progenie que hace la luz del
        mundo.

Praised be the old land the color of
          excrement,
its cavities, its sacrosanct ovaries,
the storehouses of wisdom that contained
copper, oil, magnets, ironworks, purity.
The lightning bolt that seemed to fall from
          hell
was hoarded by the ancient mother of
          roots
and each day bread came out to greet us,
unperturbed by the blood and death
          we humans wear,
the accursed progeny who deliver light
          unto the world.

Los Invitados

The Guests

Y nosotros los muertos, los escalonados
        en el tiempo,
sembrados en cementerios utilitarios y
        arrogantes
o caídos en hueseras de pobres bolivianos,
nosotros, los muertos de 1925, 26,
33, 1940, 1918, mil novecientos cinco,
mil novecientos mil, en fin, nosotros,
los fallecidos antes de esta estúpida cifra
en que ya no vivimos, qué pasa con
        nosotros?

And we the dead, distributed
        in time,
sown in utilitarian and arrogant
        cemeteries
or fallen into bone pits for poor Bolivians,
we, the dead of 1925, 26,
33, 1940, 1918, nineteen hundred and five,
nineteen hundred and a thousand, in short, we,
who died prior to this absurd number
when we are no longer alive, what becomes of
        us?

Yo, Pedro Páramo, Pedro Semilla, Pedro
     Nadie,
es que no tuve derecho a cuatro números
     y a la resurrección?
Yo quiero ver a los resurrectos para
     escupirles la cara,
a los adelantados que están a punto de
     caer
en aviones, ferrocarriles, en las guerras
     del odio,
los que apenas tuvieron tiempo de nacer y
     presentar
armas al nuevo siglo y quedarán
     tronchados,
pudriéndose en la mitad de los festejos y
     del vino!

I, Pedro Páramo, Pedro Seed, Pedro
        Nobody,
is it that I had no right to four numbers
        and to the resurrection?
I want to see the resurrected so I can
        spit in their faces,
those ahead of their time who are about to
        fall
in airplanes, trains, in wars
        of hatred,
those who scarcely had time to be born and
        to present
arms to the new century, and who will end by
        being cut down,
rotting in the midst of the festivities and
        wine!

Quiero salir de mi tumba, yo muerto, por
        qué no?

Por qué los prematuros van a ser
        olvidados?
Todos son invitados al convite!

Es un año más, es un siglo más, con
        muertos y vivos,
y hay que cuidar el protocolo, poner no
        sólo la vida,
sino las flores secas, las coronas podridas,
        el silencio,
porque el silencio tiene derecho a la
        hermosura
y nosotros, diputados de la muerte,
queremos existir un solo minuto florido
cuando se abran las puertas del honor
        venidero!

I want to leave my grave — I, a dead man —
      why not?

Why do those born before their time go on
      being forgotten?
Everyone is invited to the party!

It is one more year, one more century, with
      the dead and the living,
and we have to set the protocol, arranging
      not only life,
but the withered flowers, the rotten crowns,
      and the silence,
because the silence also has a right to know
      beauty
and we, death's representatives,
we want to exist for one single flowering moment
when the doors to a future with dignity and honor
      open!

Los Hombres

The Men

Yo soy Ramón González Barbagelata, de
      cualquier parte,
de Cucuy, de Paraná, de Río Turbio, de
      Oruro,
de Maracaibo, de Parral, de Ovalle, de
      Loncomilla,
tanto da, soy el pobre diablo del pobre
      Tercer Mundo,
el pasajero de tercera instalado, Jesús!,
en la lujosa blancura de las cordilleras
      nevadas,
disimulado entre las orquídeas de fina
      idiosincracia.

I am Ramón González Barbagelata, from
    somewhere or other,
from Cucuy, from Paraná, from Río Turbio, from
    Oruro,
from Maracaibo, from Parral, from Ovalle, from
    Loncomilla —
who cares — I am the poor bastard of the poor
    Third World,
the third-class passenger, Jesus!, settled
    down comfortably
in the luxurious whiteness of snow-covered
    mountain ranges,
hidden amidst the delicate idiosyncrasy of
    orchids.

He llegado a este mentado año 2000, y
    qué saco,
con qué me rasco, qué tengo yo que ver
con los tres ceros que se ostentan
    gloriosos
sobre mi propio cero, sobre mi
    inexistencia?
Ay de aquel corazón que esperó su
    bandera
o del hombre enramado por el amor más
    tierno,
hoy no queda sino mi vago esqueleto,
mis ojos desquiciados frente al tiempo
    inicial.

I have arrived at this esteemed year 2000, and
        what is here for me?
With what is there to scratch away the fleas? What
do these three zeros that display themselves gloriously
        over my own zero,
over my inexistence, have to do
        with me?
Aiee! that heart that awaited its
        flag
or this man embowered by a love
        more tender,
today only my idle skeleton remains,
my eyes unhinged before Inaugural
        Time.

Tiempo inicial: son estos barracones
       perdidos,
estas pobres escuelas, éstos aún harapos,
esta inseguridad terrosa de mis pobres
       familias,
esto es el día, el siglo inicial, la puerta
       de oro?

Yo, por lo menos, sin hablar de más,
       vamos, callado
como fui en la oficina, remendado y
       absorto,
proclamo lo superfluo de la inauguración:
aquí llegué con todo lo que anduvo
       conmigo,
la mala suerte y los peores empleos,
la miseria esperando siempre de par en
       par,
la movilización de la gente hacinada
y la geografía numerosa del hambre.

Inaugural Time: still there are these
       lost peasant huts,
these poor schools, yes, still these rags,
this earthly insecurity of my humble
       families:
is this the day, the inaugural century, the golden
       doorway?

I — for one, without running off at the mouth,
       let's just say, silent
like I was in the office, mended and
       absorbed —
I proclaim the inauguration to be superfluous:
I arrived here with all that travelled
       with me,
misfortune and the worst jobs,
misery always waiting with its arms
       wide open,
the mobilization of the heaped up masses
and the many many geographies of hunger.

Los Otros Hombres

The Other Men

En cambio yo, pecador pescador,
ex vanguardero ya pasado de moda,
de aquellos años muertos y remotos
hoy estoy a la entrada del milenio,
anarcopitalista furibundo,
dispuesto a dos carrillos a morder
la manzana del mundo.

On the other hand, I, a sinning fisherman,
ex-member of the now outmoded vanguard,
from those dead and distant years,
today I am at the entrance to the millennium,
a furious anarcho-capitalist,
ready to bite into and devour
the apple of the world.

Edad más floreciente ni Florencia
conoció, más florida que Florida,
más Paraíso que Valparaíso.
Yo respiro a mis anchas
en el jardín bancario de este siglo
que es por fin una gran cuenta corriente
en que por suerte soy acreedor.
Gracias a la inversión y subversión
haremos más higiénica esta edad,
ninguna guerra colonial tendrá este
       nombre
tan desacreditado y repetido,
la democracia pulverizadora
se hará cargo del nuevo diccionario:
es bello este 2000 igual al 1000:
los tres ceros iguales nos resguardan
de toda insurrección innecesaria.

Not even Florence knew a more flourishing
Age, more flowering than Florida,
more Paradise than Valparaíso.
Now I can now breathe comfortably
in the financial garden of this century
that is finally a great bank account
in which I am, luckily, a creditor.
Thanks to investment and to subversion
we will make this Age more sanitary,
no war will bear this so discredited
       and so
often repeated name: Colonial War.
Democracy, the great pulverizer,
will be in charge of the new dictionary:
this 2000, like 1000, is beautiful:
these three equal zeros safeguard us
from every unnecessary insurrection.

Los Materiales

The Materials

El mundo se llenó de sinembargos,
de infundados temores y dolor,
pero hay que reconocer que sobre el pan
      salobre
o junto a tal o cual iniquidad
los vegetales, cuando no fueron quemados,
siguieron floreciendo y repartiendo
y continuaron su trabajo verde.

The world is full of howevers,
of unfounded fears and pain,
yet we must recognize that on salted
        bread
or next to this or that inequity
the vegetables, when they weren't burnt,
continued flourishing and sharing
and continued their green work.

No hay duda que la tierra
entregó a duras penas otras cosas
de su baúl que parecía eterno:
muere el cobre, solloza el manganeso,
el petróleo es un último estertor,
el hierro se despide del carbón,
el carbón ya cerró sus cavidades.

Ahora este siglo debe asesinar
con otras máquinas de guerra, vamos
a inaugurar la muerte de otro modo,
movilizar la sangre en otras naves.

There is no doubt that the earth
through hard labor delivered other things
from its seemingly eternal womb:
the copper dies, the manganese sobs,
the oil is a final death rattle,
the iron bids farewell to the coal,
the coal has now closed its cavities.

Now this century must murder
with other war machines: let us
inaugurate death by other means,
mobilize blood on other ships.

Celebración

Celebration

Pongámonos los zapatos, la camisa listada,
el traje azul aunque ya brillen los codos,
pongámonos los fuegos de bengala y de
      artificio,
pongámonos vino y cerveza entre el cuello
      y los pies,
porque debidamente debemos celebrar
este número inmenso que costó tanto
      tiempo,
tantos años y días en paquetes,
tantas horas, tantos millones de minutos,
vamos a celebrar esta inauguración.

Let us put on our shoes, the pin-striped shirt,
the blue suit though it shines from long wear,
let us light the flares and set off
          fireworks,
let the wine and beer flow from our necks
          to our toes,
because duly we must celebrate
this immense number that cost so much
          time,
so many years and days in bundles,
so many hours, so many millions of minutes:
let us celebrate this inauguration.

Desembotellemos todas las alegrías
        resguardadas
y busquemos alguna novia perdida
que acepte una festiva dentellada.
Hoy es. Hoy ha llegado. Pisamos el tapiz
del interrogativo milenio. El corazón, la
        almendra
de la época creciente, la uva definitiva
irá depositándose en nosotros,
y será la verdad tan esperada.

Mientras tanto una hoja del follaje
acrecienta el comienzo de la edad:
rama por rama se cruzará el ramaje,
hoja por hoja subirán los días
y fruto a fruto llegará la paz:
el árbol de la dicha se prepara
desde la encarnizada raíz que sobrevive
buscando el agua, la verdad, la vida.

Let us unleash all our bottled up
        happiness
and seek out some lost sweetheart
who accepts a festive nibble.
It is today. Today has arrived. Let us
        walk on the rug
of the inquiring millennium. The heart,
        the almond
of the mounting epoch, the definitive grape
will go on depositing themselves in us,
and truth — so long awaited — will arrive.

Meanwhile, one leaf of foliage
advances the beginning of the Age:
branch by branch the trees will intertwine,
leaf by leaf the days will mount up,
and fruit by fruit peace will arrive:
the tree of happiness is prepared
from the struggling bloodroot that survives
searching for water, truth, life.

Hoy es hoy. Ha llegado este mañana
preparado por mucha oscuridad:
no sabemos si es claro todavía
este mundo recién inaugurado:
lo aclararemos, lo oscureceremos
hasta que sea dorado y quemado
como los granos duros del maíz:
a cada uno, a los recién nacidos,
a los sobrevivientes, a los ciegos,
a los mudos, a mancos y cojos,
para que vean y para que hablen,
para que sobrevivan y recorran,
para que agarren la futura fruta
del reino actual que dejamos abierto
tanto al explorador como a la reina,
tanto al interrogante cosmonauta
como al agricultor tradicional,
a las abejas que llegan ahora
para participar en la colmena

Today is today. This morning has arrived
prepared through much darkness:
still we don't know if this newly
inaugurated world is bright:
let us brighten it, let us darken it
till it is golden and burnt
like hardened grains of corn:
that each one, the newborns,
the survivors, the blind,
the mute, the maimed and crippled,
may see and may speak,
that they may survive and wander freely,
that they may seize hold of the future fruit
born of the present kingdom that we leave open
as much to the explorer as to the queen,
as much to the inquisitive cosmonaut
as to the traditional farmer,
to the bees that now arrive
to participate in the work of the hive

y sobre todo a los pueblos recientes,
a los pueblos crecientes desde ahora
con las nuevas banderas que nacieron
en cada gota de sangre o sudor.

Hoy is hoy y ayer se fue, no hay duda.

Hoy es también mañana, y yo me fui
con algún año frío que se fue,
se fue conmigo y me llevó aquel año.

De esto no cabe duda. Mi osamenta
consistió, a veces, en palabras duras
como huesos al aire y a la lluvia,
y pude celebrar lo que sucede
dejando en vez de canto o testimonio
un porfiado esqueleto de palabras.

and, above all, to the peoples newly arrived,
to the peoples increasing from now on
with new flags that were born
in each drop of blood or sweat.

Today is today and yesterday passed, this is certain.

Today is also tomorrow, and I left
with some cold year that passed,
that year left with me and took me with it.

About this there can be no doubt. My skeleton
consisted, at times, in words hard
as bones exposed to the air and rain,
and I was able to celebrate what is happening
leaving behind instead of a song or testimony
an enduring skeleton of stubborn words.